Poetry With A Purpose

Poetry for imperfect people

L. Joan Teran

authorHOUSE®

AuthorHouse™
1663 Liberty Drive
Bloomington, IN 47403
www.authorhouse.com
Phone: 1-800-839-8640

First published by AuthorHouse 6/6/2011

ISBN: 978-1-4567-3215-8 (sc)

Contents

Acknowledgment

I wish to thank Darlene McCrae, Linda Shallomuller and my Friday night prayer group for encouraging and exhorting me to finish this book. I believe what I have put down in these pages will help people have a pleasant experience during their quiet moments. This is my first poetry since I was in college in the 80's. I have awakened in the early hours with thoughts from God to put into a finished work of art. I am happy He ruled and not me because now it is finished and ready to give as a gift. You may want to take one poem a day and think about its message. I am delighted to give you this unique poetry to ponder

Introduction
Poetry With A Purpose

This is not a poetry book like any other that you would expect. It has a different twist. It will bring joy to the Christian and make others who are not certain what they do believe in to ponder. I have used different styles of writing poetry I have learned so some will be different in context and style. Some of these poems are meant to wake up the slumbering church and give them a desire to share these thoughts with others. Others of you will think it is about time someone put these subjects in poetic form. Whatever way you look at what I have written, I hope you come away with some fresh insight and spiritual revelation. Use them for a discussion group.

Forward

Many people have never sat down and gleaned through poetry as a learning tool or something they can learn new insights from. They think of it as relaxing entertainment. However, there is much you can learn from reading these pages that will make you get a fresh insight into the culture of today's world. I hope that you will not only learn by what I have written, but you will also be refreshed in your spiritual walk with God. I hope some of the poems and spiritual inspirations will bring a smile to your face. I put my heart into this for you to see how valuable you are to our Master.

One Life Restored

Two girls are going about their day,
They are laughing and full of joy,
They have just found a new place to play,
And have a brand new toy,
On this fine day
When I was on my way to work,
I stopped by a candy store,
This man sitting outside began to snore,
Why are you here in the morning?,
He replied, "to sing a song of warning ",
I frowned at him,
I doubt that he had any talent within,
Sing your song old man,
Or did you have another plan?
He sang with sweetness in his voice,
About how in life he had made a choice,
He was a follower of the lamb of God,
He had been long upon this earth,
He gave me a wink and happy nod,
He asked "do you know your true worth?",

"Of course", "I am the top CEO in my company,
They cannot make any decisions without me",
His eyes pierced through my façade,
He knew in life I did not have God,
He took my hand and looked in my eyes,
His comment took me by surprise,
"Are you sure everything is in the pink?",
What he said made me stop and think,
"You do not know anything about me,
You are just here to be in my way",

One life restored

He said, " there a possibility you don't see,
That you have lost your will to pray?",
I frowned at him, "I asked with a frown,
Aren't you that new beggar in town?",
"You forgot long ago" he replied,
"It was for you I gave up my life and died",
I turned back to answer the man again,
He had made me think about my sin,
Where did he go? I looked around,
He was singing with a heavenly sound,
I felt my heart begin to pound,
There was a new ugly sound,
I was not ready to die,
I had not prepared to meet God in the sky,
I frantically looked in every direction,
For the man who knew my imperfection?
He was no where in sight,
For my life I began to fight,
"Lord", I cried out "where are you?"
I am no good, I have sinned
And forgot about you many years,
I do not deserve salvation it is true.
I have done nothing for you I know,
But would you give me one more chance?"
Then my tears began to flow.
"For you, I want to do a victory dance."
I gave a deep gasp!,
I heard a trumpet blast,
"Today I give my life to you, my Lord,
You will be first and not last,"

Salvation Is For Everyone

For God so loved the world that he gave his only begotten Son, that whosoever believes in him, should not perish but have everlasting life. John 3:16 The persons who received John the Baptist's testimony regarding Jesus also were prepared to receive Jesus teaching.

God's word says it this way: "for He whom God has sent speaks the words of God, for God does not give the Spirit by measure. The Father loves the Son and has given all things into his hands. He who believes in the Son has everlasting life; and he who does not believe the Son shall not see life, but the wrath of God abides on him." John 3:34-36

As you ponder about this, I hope you make the decision to follow Jesus as your savior and Lord. I, like many, loved Jesus with all my heart when I was a child, but strayed away for a season. Now I am a sold out believer and intend to spend my life living for him. He is awesome!

Without Him I am nothing. The poems say it well. Use them to persuade others the reason why Jesus came to earth, and to know His resurrection power is available for everyone.

.

One New Man

I woke up in time
To hear this rhyme
It was going along well,
Until he started to yell hell,
I was here to play,
I did not want to hear about God today,
As the gaudy haggard man went on talking,
I sped up my walking,
He shouted "You see my friend,
I have some advice to lend,
If you think you can live your own way,
You will have to pay for it some day,"
I laughed within myself,
"You mean take my bible off the shelf?",
I had not one of those to read,
I had sold it to a friend for a bag of weed,
It had been so very long,
I did not even remember right from wrong,
I tried not to listen,
As he told about his folly,
Then suddenly his face became sad,
He told how he had been a bad dad,
He was rough and tough,
But his son saw through his bluff,
My son said, "Dad, I'm tired of your blarney,
It'd be nice if we had some harmony,
You have lied and cheated, left us alone,
So to your familiar haunts you could roam",
He said,, "I never cared if they were happy,
I never knew how to be a good pappy,

My soul was tainted, I was going to hell,
And that his son knew quite well,
Some preacher came to their town,
When he met this man he gave a frown,
Everyone else he thought he could fool,
But this man had a bible as his tool,

His son had asked him to go to church,
He went with him and come in with a lurch,
This preacher he could not leave behind.,
His face and message was too kind,
He taught them about the prodigal son,
And I realized that I was one,
I began to have tears come to my eyes,
This must have been to my son a surprise,
The prodigal son's father represented God,
Jesus one day had walked upon this sod,
My sins he could wash away
Because my sins debt he did pay,
I wanted to run away and forget about his word,
Yet I wanted to stay and hear more about this man's Lord,
He began to laugh and hit his hand against his knee,
He said, "Jesus died upon the cross just for you and me",

One foot was ready to run away in a hurry,
The other joined in this man's story,
I wanted to feel clean and free,
I was tired of always feeling so empty,
The man gave an altar call,
Each person listening in line did fall,
They wanted to know Jesus as their Lord,
I slowly turned to join them in one accord,

One new man

I have never missed my old life of sin,
I have been too busy other souls to win,
Now my son looks at me with a smile,
"Dad I sure like your new lifestyle",
God pursued and wooed me,
I came to my senses in time,
Jesus hung on the tree for me,
Now I keep step to His rhyme,
I am happy in my new life,
I no longer live in constant strife,
I am privileged to be,
That one new man you see

Some Thoughts To Ponder

Abraham believed God, and it was reckoned to him for righteousness. Blessed are we whose iniquities are forgiven and whose sins are covered. Blessed is the person to whom the Lor d will not regard his sins. Therefore, we are purified by the blood of Jesus. Our past sins are not calculated and held in account against us when we become a follower Jesus.

To the pure all things are pure; but left on our own we cannot see things pure. We cannot live a life of purity with a purpose to solely follow in God's ways. Adam's disobedience rendered all future descendents to be born in sin.

The law that came in caused us to recognize how sinful we were. No person was able to keep the law. But, where sin abounded, the loving-kindness of God was lavished the more. Just as sin had reigned through death; so also grace does rule as king in righteousness, which results in eternal life.

Sin once was the master of all mankind. Now grace is the ruling factor with Christ's righteousness as it's purpose. It makes us be as if we had never sinned because of Christ's sinless life and, crucifixion and resurrection paying our sin debt.

This does not give you a license to keep sinning. You need to get to know your new master Jesus. You once obeyed Satan and done things your own way. Study God's word to show yourself approved unto God, which is your reasonable service. Read Romans 5 and ponder on what these truths means to you as a believer in Christ.

Surpise Me

I climbed the stair,
The day was fair,
I had accomplished my work,
Without a single quirk.
I sat at my table,
Staring out the window nearby,
I felt unstable,
And wondered why.
As the day went on,
I thought of my son,
He was gone away,
And there would stay.
I was full of memories,
Some were sad,
Some made me glad,
There were so many stories.
The phone then rang,
Someone came in with a big bang,
When I looked up, it was him,
My son stood by me trying to look grim.
He asked me to forgive him,
Because me he did not obey,
Of course, I said,
I thought you were dead.
He kept his head down,
And looked at me with a frown,
Then he broke out in laughter,
You can know I am ready for the hereafter?

Surprise me

We spent a happy time together,
I forgot I had been under the weather,
There was joy in the air,
And much love to spare.

We Are A New Creation

Jesus made us one new man because of the sacrifice he offered up for us. We could not save ourselves because we were clothed in Adam's sinful flesh. Jesus was spotless and blameless. Adam's disobedience brought death upon all mankind. Jesus made us purified. By his dying for the transgressions of the law, he made us justified in God's sight. (Romans 5:8-19)

"By his dying, he offered one sacrifice for sins for all time. At his resurrection, he sat down at the right hand of God, waiting from that time onward until his enemies be made a footstool for His feet. (Psalm 110:1-3) For by one offering he has perfected for all time those who are sanctified." (Hebrews 10:12-22).

Please read John 16:4-11. At this time Jesus introduced his disciples to the trinity as he alone knew it. When he arose to be with the Father, the Holy Spirit was sent to guide them and live in those who believe in Jesus Christ as their Lord and Savior.

The trinity shows us God's perfect balance and order. The Father and Son were co-creators of the universe. Psalm 95:6-7 tells us, "Come let us bow down in worship, let us kneel before the Lord our Maker, for he is our God and we are the people of his pasture, the flock under his care."

When God created the world, after each thing that he substance produced, he said, "It is good or very good." After he created man he said, It is not good (for man to be alone). (Genesis 2:22-25). It interfered with his perfection of the trinity; the Father, Son and Holy Spirit. After Eve was created, God commanded "Be fruitful and multiply; fill the earth and subdue it." This would be putting things in God's order of the trinity.

Jesus told his disciples before he ascended in John 14:15-16,20 "If you love me, you will obey what I command. And I will ask the Father, and he will give you another counselor to be with you forever - the Spirit of truth. The world cannot accept him, because it neither sees him nor knows him. But you know him, for he lives with you and will be in you. On that day you will realize that I am in my Father and you are in me, and I am in you." What an awesome thought and even fearful because The Holy Spirit is the part of the Godhead that is living in us.

Ephesians 1:13-14 says, "And you also were included in Christ when you heard the word of truth, the gospel of your salvation. Having believed in him you were marked by him with a seal, the promised Holy Spirit, who is a deposit guaranteeing our inheritance until the redemption of those who are God's possession - to the praise of his glory."

Read Ephesians 2:4-10 you will see that it is by God's grace we become God's workmanship. We are part of his order in the trinity. The Father loves the Son; the Son submits to the Father and the Holy Spirit is an expression of them just as a child is the asseveration of their father and mother. The child did nothing to be born. It was because the mother conceived the father's sperm. Neither can we work out our own salvation by any works we do that will help us be a part of the purposes of God in the trinity.

We are a new creation

Read Ephesians 2:13-18. We have access to the Father by the blood of Jesus and the Holy Spirit. Jesus is our bond of peace between the Father and us. By his sacrifice, he removed the hostility of the Law, with all its commandments and rules. We don't need to struggle to please God. It is through Jesus that we, Jews and Gentiles alike, are united in the one Spirit. We are now able to approach the heavenly Father. We, who believe in Christ, should make a definite determination to follow God by submitting to the Holy Spirit's guidance that dwells in us, Jesus submits to the Father; The Father works together with the Son. Jesus did not want us to struggle on our own so the Holy Spirit was given to us as our helper when he ascended.

Ephesians 5:1-2 says, "Be imitators of God, therefore, as dearly loved children and live a life of love, just as Christ loved us and gave himself up for us as a fragrant offering and sacrifice to God."

The old covenant had its rules and ordinances for public worship. Only priests could go behind the second veil into the holy of holies. Once a year the priest offered a blood sacrifice for himself and the people. In the old covenant, the Israelites had very specific sacrifices and offerings that they were required to do on a regular basis. If they did not do them, they could have been put out of the camp.

Jesus went out of the camp by coming down to earth from heaven to pay the price for our sins on the cross, and make us a brand new creation.

(2 Corinthians 5:17)

We are a new creation

We read in Hebrews 9:1-15; 12:24 that at the appointed time Christ, the Messiah, appeared as High Priest. By his own blood, Christ entered into heaven - the true Holy of Holies in his resurrected body. He had no spot or blemish. He made it possible for us to be justified in God's sight. It is just as if we have never sinned when we accept Christ Jesus finished work on the cross. Jesus is the mediator of the new covenant. He ushered in the new covenant that we live under.

There is no room for pride. We are God's own handiwork. He has created us and made our union in Christ Jesus his pledge to us so we will perform good deeds from the heart, and not because of obligation. We have become a holy priesthood to offer up spiritual sacrifices acceptable to God by Jesus Christ.

We are a chosen generation, a royal priesthood, and a people proclaimed by God as his own people and possession. Our part is to praise him and tell others about his wonderful deeds and the redemption that he has offered us.

(see I Peter 2:9-10) We are to study the scriptures to learn how we should live as being a new creation.

The Lord has lavished his love upon us by calling us his sons and daughters. (see I John 3:1-3) The Holy Spirit will help us learn about the trinity so we can KNOW the Father, Son and Holy Spirit. When someone wants to refer to your past sins, remind them you are a blood bought child of God. The old has passed away and the new has come.

We are a new creation

You may want to read all of Hebrews 9 and 10 to get a full understanding of the difference between the Old Covenant, also called the testament, and the new covenant that we live under. Read I Peter 2:5-9; I John 3:1-2.

The Day Of The Reaper

Some of our habits
Tell us them to obey.
Yet within us a new voice speaks,
Saying "throw all that garbage away."
Why do we halt and listen?
Then just simply turn away,
Our own selfish desires beckoning within,
Saying "I don't want to today"?
After we are older, we will get bolder
We will not than run away.
Instead our heart grows colder,
Jesus name we hardly say.
Tomorrow may be the day of the reaper,
I am fearful and still
I have never been a covenant keeper.
It is always follow my own will.
I will take a stand some day,
What else can I say?,
Perhaps I will fumble and bumble,
But for Jesus can I really be humble? .

Time goes on,
Now the grave is at my doorstep
I hustled and bustled my life through,
Now my love for Jesus is no longer true.
I heard a rumble within and without,
"You fool today your soul
Will be required of you,"
I heard with a shout.
Repent of your sin
And your pride

The day of the reaper

God wants to come by your side,
Be pleased to know he wants in.

Hells' doors are beckoning me,
I have yearned to be free,
Now I realize a trap I myself set,
And the choice to follow is not yet.
My heart pounded hard,
The whole house was jarred,
I bellowed out "Jesus not now."
And before Him I did bow.
He asked, "what have you done,
How many souls have you won?",
I said, "none Lord,
With you I was bored".
I said, "I will come when I am older."
He said, "come, lean on my shoulder."
I replied, "that is borrowing much sorrow,
Come on back tomorrow."
He said, "I know my son,
Your life has always been undone,
You fought to keep self,
God's word stayed on the shelf,

Some people worship me as Lord of all
Each one has a choice to answer my call,
Others kneel before me as judge,
Not everyone towards me will budge,
Now bow your knee, my son,
For you, I am judge you see,
The days of your choices are done,
You will forever be separated from me."

The day of the reaper

I began to cry aloud,
No, God, just one more chance
I sunk out of His sight,
Never getting a second glance,
I had chosen my destiny,
Now I was in agony,
The day of the reaper
Had come to me.

Our Weakest Point

The devil always hits us at our weakest point. His power is elevated in our weakness. When we think we are strong in an area, it could be true. It also could be that the deceiver is taking us when we are off guard to an old weak area subtly. We think we have overcome but the familiar spirit tries to take us off track again. If we resist and remain strong, we will gain the victory. This takes knowing which voice we are hearing. Is it the Lord's voice or a demonic spirit or our own flesh?

When the good times roll, it com-forts us. We need to be thankful to our provider. Any time we think we had the victory on our own, we open the door to rebellion and an independent spirit. We are dependent on our Lord, who supplies all our needs.

Looking to Him for strength, also will help us have more strength for the hard times and temptations. Trials help us to develop character.

My brethren, count it all joy when ye fall into divers temptations: knowing this, that the trying of your faith worketh patience. But let patience have her perfect work, that ye may be perfect and entire, wanting nothing. (James 1:2-4 KJV)

Hither And Yon

When you have traveled the world o'er
And gone from shore to shore,
Trying to fill empty places
Making happy the sad faces,
You will go from here to there,
Always finding your soul bare,
Saying "I will do fine for today,
No use begging for tomorrow anyway",
Fill that empty space
Let it be a happy place,
Let Jesus come into your heart,
Giving your life a new start,
After all is said and done,
You are the only one to choose,
When Jesus you will see,
Whether your judge or savior he will be.

The God Of The Impossible

"For I will pour water on him that is thirsty, and floods upon the dry ground: I will pour my spirit upon thy seed, and my blessings upon thine offspring."

(Isaiah 44:3)

There is no problem that he cannot solve. There is no question that he cannot answer. There is no disease that he cannot heal. There is no demon that he cannot cast out. There is no enemy that he cannot defeat - the battle is the Lord's. There is no difficulty that he can not overcome. There is no bondage that he cannot break. There is no prison door that he cannot open. There is no need that he cannot meet. There is no mountain that he cannot move.

In fact, Jesus said " *if ye have faith as a grain of mustard seed, ye shall say unto this mountain, remove hence to yonder place; and it shall remove; and nothing shall be impossible unto you.*" (Read Matthew 17:14-21)

The God who shut the mouth of the lions in the den, where Daniel was thrown, can also stop the mouth of those who speak against you. (Daniel 6:20-23; Isaiah 54:17)

The God who delivered Shadrach, Meshach, and Abednego out of the fiery furnace can deliver you out of your trials and temptations. (Daniel 3:26-30; Romans 8:38-39)

Jesus, who turned the water into wine at the wedding feast, can turn your crises into a miracle. (John 2:1-11)

The God who compelled the pairs of animals, birds, etc. to come to the ark before the flood can speak to people and draw them to your business or to help you in time of need; as well as to use you to bring them to salvation in Christ. (Genesis 7:20-21; John 6:44)

The God of the impossible

The God who filled the temple of Solomon with the glory cloud can fill you with his Holy Spirit and empower you to do his will. (I Kings 8:10-11; Acts 1:8)

"Whom have I in heaven but you? And there is none upon the earth that I desire besides you. My flesh and my heart fail; but God is the strength of my heart and my portion forever." (Psalm 73:25-26)

Don't Be Fooled By Me

Don't be fooled by the face I wear,
I wear a thousand masks
Masks that I am afraid to take off
And none of them are me,
Pretending is second nature to me,
I give the impression that I am secure,
That all is sunny and unruffled
Within and without,
That confidence is my name
And coolness is my game,
That the waters calm
and I am in command,
My surface may seem smooth,
And that I need no one;
But my surface is my mask,
Beneath dwells the real me in fear,
With Confusion and aloneness within,
Afraid I am not perfect and wise,
But I hide this to shield me
From the glance that knows who I am,

But such a glance is precisely what I need,
If it is followed by acceptance and love,
It can assure me
Of what I cannot assure myself,
I am afraid that deep down I am no good,
That I am nothing, and you will see this
I need to know I am worth something,
So I play my game, my desperate game,
I begin a parade of masks,
And life for me becomes a play,

Don't be fooled by me

Idly I chatter to you in suave tones
Of surface talk,
Don't be fooled by what I say,
I tell you everything that is really nothing,
And nothing of what is everything
While crying inside,
Please listen carefully to hear
What I am not saying,
What I am not able to say
But would like to,
What for survival I need to say,
But CAN'T.

Don't be fooled by me,
Look beyond my masks

The Great Exchange

Jesus gave more than a kiss, he gave his life for our salvation and redemption. Redemption means that Jesus can put into anyone the hereditary nature that was in himself. All the standards he gave us are based on his nature. His teaching is meant to be applied to the life he put within us when we became born again. Our part is simply to agree with his verdict of sin as judged on the cross of Christ redemption.

Say "I am happy in God, my Lord, who brought me out of the mire and muck and placed my feet on solid ground. He took my hand and led me. When I pass through the waters, I will not drown. When I pass through the fire I will not be burned." (See Isaiah 43:1-2)

When we come into this world, we all have a blank slate. We are born in sin because Adam's nature is within us. It is up to us what we put on our life slate. We can accept Jesus as Lord and he will be our guide; or we can try to do things our own

way and in the end lose eternal life.

When Jesus died for us, we have been given THE WAY to follow.(John 14:6) We need to die to our "self" and let God be in control. We will not worry what others think of us when we are walking with the Lord. He has done the great exchange for us to be worthy to inherit not only his nature, but eternal life as well.

Jesus gave more than a kiss, he gave us his beauty. He paid more than a visit, he paid for our mistakes on the cross. He took more than a minute, he took away our sin and wants to be our savior.

The great exchange

What an awesome Lord we serve. He didn't deserve the rejection he received. We don't deserve his extravagant love. God always breaks into our lives in unusual ways. We can't tell God how to make things work out. Flow with the Holy Spirit and let him guide you.

Don't always want to know how the movie of your life is going to end. We need to live our life knowing God has our best interest in mind.

We cannot expect God to be on our timetable. God uses our failures as a foundation for his successes.

God moves in mysterious ways his wonders to perform. As we surrender to put Jesus first, we will learn how much he loves us more clearly. Read Psalm 139 When we feel like nobody knows who we are or cares about us, we will learn that he knows all about us (even before we were born). It is awesome! We don't have to wear a mask

Joy Comes In The Morning

Joy comes in the morning
But can it stay all day?
Joy comes in the evening,
And the joy has never gone away,
I am a child of God,
I walk with purpose upon this sod,
My life is filled with love from my King,
It is worth giving him my everything,
Even though the times might get tough,
God's with me in that kind of stuff,
Take delight in the hard times too,
For they are meant to refine you,
Have joy when the good times are returned
Thank God for the things you have learned,
It will equip you for the final days,
God was always there, give him praise,
Be ready for the end times too,
Jesus will soon be returning for you,
We will see him coming in clouds above,
To prove to his followers his great love,

He is coming back to rule as our King,
I want to be there more than anything,
I count the days until Jesus I see,
I will be with him for all eternity,
Take a stand today my friend,
Do not wait until your bitter end,
Don't think hell is not real,
Satan's lies are so your life he can steal,
He is coming soon friend, do not delay,
It is now that the gospel you must obey,

Joy in the morning

He has loved you with an everlasting love,
Don't reject him or give him a shove,
I will have a place to fulfill all my destiny,
That he has planned for me to ascribe,
Come today to join his family,
Leave behind your selfish pride.
Delight when he takes you with him home,
May he also take your loved ones too,
If they thought they could delay,
They'll end up in judgment on that last day

Father Knows Me

After you have tried every thing else, are you willing to stop a moment and see that there is only one Almighty God? He really understands you. He knows all about you and still wants you as his child. He does see your flaws and stubborn heart, but beyond that, he sees your potential. No one has any excuse for overlooking their maker and serving other gods.

We can lose our great job. We can have betrayal by friends. We can have tragedy happen to us. If we know about Jesus and the cross, we will have the strength to go through tough times. We will be grateful for the tender moments. It all depends on how we perceive the price Jesus paid for us on the cross.

Oh Lord, thou hast searched me and known me. Thou knowest my down sitting and mine uprising, thou art acquainted with all my ways. For there is not a word on my tongue, but, lo O Lord, thou knowest it altogether. (Psalm 139:1-4)

Reconciliation

I climbed the stair,
The day was fair,
I had accomplished my work,
Without a single quirk,
I sat at the table
Staring out the window at people nearby,
I felt unstable,
And wondered why,
As the day went on,
I thought of my son,
He was gone away,
And there would stay,
I counted my memory glories,
Some were sad,
Some made me glad,
There were so many stories,
The phone then rang,
Someone came in with a big bang,
When I answered it was him
My son stood by me with a grin,

He asked me to forgive him
He had not obeyed me,
Of course, I said,
I thought you were dead,
We laughed a lot,
We had missed one another,
More than we thought,
Our disagreements were no longer a bother

Reconciliation

He had made a new life,
His wandering was done,
He had a sweet wife,
And a wonderful son,

May Joy

May joy lie before you and trouble behind you. May good health go with you, and good fortune find you. May foes make amends and friendships continue. May love walk beside you and peace live within you.

He who believes in Jesus will have living water flow from his heart. We have nothing to do with the outflow. It is the work of God. The rivers of the Holy Spirit overcomes obstacles in our way. He is our guide.

I Am Alive

Life is meant to abundantly live,
Not let old age steal your joy,
Why should I just sit and knit,
When I have so much to give?
Who said getting old was a drag?
About my age I do brag,
I walk and daily exercise,
To some people that is a great surprise,
Sometimes I get stiff as a board,
But with others I am in one accord,
As long as I am alive and can do it,
I will live each day as if I was up to it,
Now you young people listen to me,
Positive attitude is the key,
When things go wrong, and they often will,
Look up to Jesus, your heart he will still.

What Are They Up To?

Today the child is left alone,
He is often on his very own,
They all have some gadget and game,
Nobody cares to keep them tame,
First they took the bible from the school,
This was applied as a God destroying tool,
They took the cross from the public square
They did not want you Jesus story to share,
Next the ten commandments must be gone,
From the court room and beyond,
Instead they wanted us to hear,
There is no need for God to appear,
They planned it so that one day,
The people would allow deceit and lies,
We'd never know it's God we should obey,
They would just make up more alibi's,
There was a small lady who stood up,
For what was right like a stubborn pup,
Each day she would walk and pray
God will come back she would say,

She set her microphone up in the square,
She felt this was only fair,
People needed to know right from wrong,
She put God's word into a special song,
Be ready, Jesus is coming back,
Change your ways today,
Do not hesitate or be slack,
Or you will never see another way.

Our School Children

Children playing with gleeful shout,
Running and jumping with no pout,
Looking for someone to share their play,
And with them a few words to say,
They hear the school bell,
And fall in line after one another,
Do they know their lessons well,
And act like sister and brother?,
One girl wears a small cross,
She loves Jesus and wants nobody lost,
The teacher yanks it from her neck,
"You know this must be kept in check",
The girl smiles and blesses her teacher,
She learned to bless from her preacher,
The teacher is puzzled at how she reacts,
Doesn't she know the government facts?,
No more can there be prayer or godly song,
Nobody can teach right from wrong,
But this girl knows Jesus inside,
And by his word and love does abide,
The teacher watched how children fought,
The one got hurt and began to cry,
The Christian girl sang a song nearby,
She practiced love as she had been taught,
Soon all children turned away,
As she began quietly to pray,
"Lord help them learn to know you,
So they won't be in such a stew",
The one who was hurt ran to the girl,
Will you please help me get well,
I am afraid of that place you call hell,

Our school children

She held his hand and gave a smile,
Today is the time to come to your savior,
He will help you out with everything,
He will teach you how to live,
And change your behavior
They laughed and played,
After the bell rang they stayed,
The classroom was different,
There was less tension and peace.

Joy Is Ours To Claim

Jesus calms the tempest of the soul,
His purpose is to make us whole,
Free at last,
With a great big blast,
Freedom heals our grief,
And brings us complete relief,
Many people look for healing,
From the spirit of infirmity stealing,
Joy comes in the morning,
But pain comes without warning,
Satan attacks are always the same,
He brings blame and shame,
Be on your guard,
It is not really hard,
Call out to Jesus in today's grief,
It will be tomorrows relief,
Jesus gives you a destination,
At the point of your salvation,
He takes the lowly, bent down
And makes a person of renown,

You are more than an overcomer,
Even when life seems like a bummer,
You can have what the bible does say,
Or have the devil to pay,
Pray, love others and God always obey
His love will find the way,
Through the mire and muck,
It doesn't come from good luck,

Joy is ours to claim

You are free my friend,
Your soul will soon mend,
Today you will see,
Jesus can help you win the victory,

The Valley He Lives In

This valley that man lives in,
Is known as the place of sin,
It is beautiful and bright,
Jesus is coming here for him tonight,
"No", said the man very loud,
"I have too much to give up,
Of my fortune I am proud,
Could you please come later?"
"No," Jesus voice spoke strong,
"It is time for you to sing a different song,
You've built your monuments and legacy,
But you never wanted any time with me.
There will be eternal separation from me,
You have made that your preparation,
You believed the lies that you have told,
Now you will leave behind all your gold,

Changing Our Live's

When we come into this world, we all have a blank slate. It is up to us what we put on it. We need God's help to erase our mistakes. Sometimes our opinion is so deeply engrained in us that it is hard to change our mindset, words and attitude. What others have said and we accepted as fact is our self talk. We can tell our self something so often we believe it.

Our mind can be so cluttered with what we think, that we forget to ask God what he thinks or what he wants us to do.

Just sitting quietly in the presence of Jesus will help unclutter our thinking. We can understand his Word better. After our quiet time, there is less bad self talk or angry irruptions at others. Therefore, it is a more balanced, attitude.

Some people will say to you "You are different. I like this new attitude better."

Have A Fun Day

I watched them play today,
They have so much to say,
Get your finger out of your nose,
You want more attention I suppose,
Laughter and cheers fill the room,
They are all filled with glee,
They have manners sometimes,
They are free to be "just me",
Sometimes we adults forget who we are,
They know they are the shinning star,
They are trying to think what they can do,
To make us get into a stew,
Mom comes into the room,
And away they zoom,
Do not forget to laugh today,
Be a simple child in some way.

Face Value

People came in and sat towards the rear,
"Ok pastor, you can see that I am here,
Let's get this over with soon,
I want to be out of here by noon."
Others came in,
These people looked battered from sin,
They looked very sad,
They knew they had been bad.
The pastor came in with his head down,
He looked around with a frown,
Who are these new people sitting here?
There's the usual ones who sit in the rear,
The band began sublime,
The new people knew this was their time,,
They were there to pray and listen,
Their faces had a happy glisten.
As time went on, they cried loudly to God,
"Come back soon Lord and walk this sod"
Applause broke out all over the place,
Soon there was not even one single space.

These people were youth from the street.
But our Master they with respect do treat,
Pastor went out as his tears began to flow,
"These youth their Lord they do know"
The pastor came back in with a smile,
He knew they would be there for awhile,
Did all the others lose their way?
Do they not want our God to obey?
They left in their heart long ago,
In their face there was no glow,

Face Value

It was just rote to them,
They never even liked to sing a hymn.
The pastor said, "I will sow the seed of God
In this new generation,
To carry it wherever they trod,
They are looking for their King

To return in celebration,
As for me,
I had almost forgotten
There was a God."
Now I ask you to decide,
Which persons had only face value,
And which ones heart had Jesus inside?

Words Of Exhortation

I would like to give you words of exhortation today. It is for everygeneration of believers, who are truly reaching out to follow God.

"Fear thou not;(there is nothing to fear) for I am with thee: (do not look around in terror) and be not dismayed, for I am thy God. I will strengthen thee; (and harden you to difficulties) Yea, I'll help thee; yea, I will uphold thee with the right hand (retain you with my victorious hand) of my righteousness (and justice)". Isaiah 41:10 (parenthesis are my thoughts)

It is by the cross that we have the door by which every human can choose to enter into the life of God. By Jesus resurrection, he has given us the right to eternal life. At his ascension, our Lord entered heaven. He is seated at the right hand of the Father God. He keeps the door open for all mankind. His prayer and posture says to us, "come now and enter in. Let us reason together. Become one with me, as I am one with the Father."

We were created for complete union with the Father, Son and Holy Spirit in intimacy. Our body and soul (which is our mind, will and emotions) is our gate to enter in.

Words of exhortation

We have five physical senses.(see, touch, taste, hear and smell); This allows us to identify with Jesus on earth in human form. With our soul, we are allowed to make choices; and with our spirit (we have the capacity to know and worship God). Let your whole being (body, soul, and spirit) worship your creator and Savior now.

Follow Me To The Cross

Follow me to the cross,
Seek your liberty,
Give Jesus your life,
With the cross he has set you free.
Are you willing to go all the way?
Are you the worker God seeks today?
Will you be faithful enough to be,
The one Jesus will set free
Are you weak enough
For your love to grow?
Are you strong enough
For your faith to show?
Can you leave your worldly style
And follow him?
Will you go one more mile
And achieve complete victory?

Follow me to the cross
Learn to live for your savior,
Stop trying to be your own boss,
So that my seed may grow in thee
Give Jesus your life,
He will live in thee,
For at the cross,
He achieved for you the victory

The Mighty One

You ride high upon the heavens,
You cover all the earth,
You have stilled the storms,
You have walked upon the water,
My heavenly Father, I come before you,
For you have said in your promises,
Wherever two or more agree,
There you will be,
Now I come before you in Jesus name,
Asking that you will answer me,
Let Jesus be the healer,
And take away the pain,
How I love and adore you,
Let your glory shine forth,
Show your power in this hour,
To let all know your fame,
I love you and I always will,
I am making this petition,
With my whole heart
I Magnify your holy name,

Prayer For Today

I pray that my love will grow stronger in personal knowledge and perception em-powering me to sense what is vital, and to learn to prize what is of value so that I can be inwardly clean; no one being able to criticize me wrongly from now until the time that the Lord returns; bearing a rich harvest of that righteousness which comes through Jesus Christ by which I can glorify and praise God. Amen

The Gangs Going Down

So you think you are bad,
That your life is a fad,
Think that you will live through the fight,
Unless you die tonight,
That old lady down the block,
Told us we were in for a shock,
Repent or you will find,
I am a woman of a different kind,
She said to us, "sit down and listen",
Her face began to glisten,
One of you might die tonight,
You need to get your life right,
We all laughed and acted cool,
Until one of us began to turn blue,
She called out to her God,
And the room began to shake,

"Boys you can change your life tonight
And learn to do what is right,
You were born with a purpose and plan,
But it is up to you to give God your hand,
You are not here just to fill a space,
God has given you a destiny,
Become what you are meant to be,
It is up to you a better way to chase",

Their leader began to cry,
Am I the one who is going to die?
He wanted her to mock,
His expression changed into a shock,
He began to breathe heavy and quick,

The gangs going down

His motions turned to a different tune
He knew his life could be over soon,
What could he do to get a quick fix?
Everyone laughed and acted tough,
Her gaze called their bluff,
The leader sat down and said "ok,
God I want to obey",
They jerked him to his feet,
"You are the biggest cheat,"
"Not anymore", she said "he chose right.
One of you will never be the same".

Anybody Can Come

If your heart is right,
And your conscience clear,
I will take you out from bondage,
To a place where you never need to fear,
You will fight your enemy,
There is where you will take your stand,
Anybody can come and be set free,
Come with me to the promised land,
You knew hard times in your slavery,
God will test you before you have victory,
You can come along with me,
God is the one who will set you free,
He will give you the cloud by day,
And the fire by night,
The Lord, will give you time to know him,
And get your heart right,
I will take you across the desert,
And through the Red Sea,
Are you willing to walk along with me?
He is the one who will give you Jubilee.

The Fire

There was a fire
Next door to me,
The old man was ready to retire,
And just be free.
He spent all his life waiting for the day
He could pick up his final pay.
Yesterday was the day to say goodbye,
Now he knows what he expected was a lie,
He wanted to set his life straight,
Maybe marry him a mate,
But he got drunk to celebrate,
And now he won't wont ever get to relate,
Where do you spend your days in life,
Is it filled with only working and strife?,
When all is said and done,
To God's salvation have you come?